THE LESSER TRAGEDY OF DEATH

THE LESSER TRAGEDY OF DEATH

OF DEATH

BY CRISTINA GARCÍA

BLACK GOAT
LOS ANGELES

BLACK GOAT is an independent poetry imprint of Akashic Books created and curated by award-winning Nigerian author Chris Abani. Black Goat is committed to publishing well-crafted poetry, focusing on experimental and thematically challenging work. The series aims to create a proportional representation of female and non-American poets, with an emphasis on Africans. Series titles include:

Gomer's Song by Kwame Dawes
The Ravenous Audience by Kate Durbin
Globetrotter & Hitler's Children by Amatoritsero Ede
Abstraktion und Einfühlung by Percival Everett
Auto Mechanic's Daughter by Karen Harryman
Controlled Decay by Gabriela Jauregui
eel on reef by Uche Nduka
Conduit by Khadijah Queen
to be hung from the ceiling by strings of varying length by Rick Reid

Published by Akashic Books
©2010 Cristina García

ISBN-13: 978-1-936070-01-5
Library of Congress Control Number: 2009939083

First printing

Black Goat
c/o Akashic Books
PO Box 1456
New York, NY 10009
info@akashicbooks.com
www.akashicbooks.com

For Paqui

Acknowledgments

Mil gracias to Dean Rader for his generosity and brilliance.

Thank you to Donna Seaman and to *Triquarterly* for publishing "Twenty-Nine Palms," and to Daniel Shapiro for including "Spell," "Brownstone," "Twenty-Nine Palms," "Namesake," and "What You Dream" in *Review 78, Literature and Arts of the Americas*. Also, my gratitude to Craig Perez and Jennifer Reimer of Achiote Press for their early support of my poetry.

And, of course, *un gran abrazo* to Chris Abani, friend without peer.

Every Angel is terrible. And yet, alas,
I sing to you . . .

— Rainer Maria Rilke

TABLE OF CONTENTS

PART III: 1995–2007

PREFACE

TAPESTRY

A salon, or sunlit rotunda (our old dining room?).
You come speak to me. People who knew you come too,
whispering things.

This business of biography is a sham.

Thin green brocade of words.
Knots of grief. Can grief be a gift?
I fear it will make me your enemy but you must

trust me: I offer this in peace.

PART I

1960–1972

WHAT YOU BELIEVE

That you can speak to dogs.
That they don't listen to you.

That women are impenetrable,
except for the obvious.

That children should like you.

That it's possible to be a hero.

That the good things in life are bad for
you: mothers, malted milk balls, cocaine.

That there is a God but He's ignored you.

That a family awaits you.

That you suffer for cheapness.
(Are you listening, Dad?)

That one morning you'll wake up dead.
And *that* will be without pain.

DESEO

To recover the lost wealth
of boyhood, to bait you
with the magic of ordinary days.

RESPUESTA

Our childhood is dead.
Nothing is left but this:

your words against mine.

WHAT TÍA CUCA SAID

That Mami asked *¿Quién es?*
when you were put in her arms.
That her teeth fell out.
That she got fat and depressed.
That three children in thirty-five
months was too much.

It's not that she rejected you,
but this:
No one thought she was pretty anymore.
No one looked at her twice.

BIENVENIDO

This was never you—
firstborn; daughter, time
standing still for pure awe.
Celebrations and party dresses,
professional photographs.

When you were born, the revolution
soured and the deluxe world we lived in
was crumbling. Who had time to welcome
one small boy?

BOY

You gave away everything:
your candy and rapt attention, the marbles
on your Chinese checkerboard.

I winced at your misplaced trust. Why couldn't you
toughen up? You were a boy, weren't you?
Where did your gentleness come from?

Mornings you woke up cheerful in your crib.
The one you slept in till you were ten.

THE TWIST

We got to working on your finger snapping
first. Until you did it without missing a beat.
Fling out your elbows!
Turn your knees to rubber!
Like your life depended on it.

We made you believe you looked
cool, *hermano*. Twitchy, pint-sized swinger,
little Cuban Elvis in short pants and a cowlick.
This was your first, your easiest
step. Chubby Checker was next.

Now, are you ready to do the twist?

KINDERGARTEN

You wore your suit like a scratchy
blanket, little bow tie and jacket,
perfectly creased long pants, a crew cut.
Crayons and Superman lunch box in hand,
you took your place with us.

Mami made sure we looked good
on the outside, that the world
would never point to us and say *less than*.
Who knew the real damage
was done on the inside?

BIKE

You begged me to teach you to ride
a two-wheeler. All the other kids
knew how. You're too short,
I said. You can't reach
the pedals. Wait till you grow.

I don't wanna wait till I grow,
you said. Please, okay? Please.
I knew better but I sat you high
on the seat, feet dangling, hands
barely grabbing the handlebars.

Whatever you do, hold on,
I advised. Ready? You nodded.
Set? You blinked, suddenly scared.
(We were atop Danger Hill.) Go!

Your tiny body flew, bump after bump,
until an eternity later, you crashed. Cut
and bleeding, you cried: But I held on!
Yes you did, I said.

BY THE SEA

By the sea, by the sea, by the beautiful sea!

Mami worked for days on your costume, a 1920s
bathing suit that came to your knees—striped, sleeveless,
with a scooped-out neck. She made you practice singing
out loud so you'd be sure to stand out.

You and me, you and me, oh how happy we'll be!

That's my son! Mami pointed you out to everyone. I
made his costume myself! How she clapped and laughed
watching you Charleston in your fake moustache. But we
still couldn't hear you sing.

I love to be beside your side, beside the sea . . .

I saw Mami hug you that night.
I saw you, shy and pleased.

EASY OUT

The one time we saw you play we were fooled
by your uniform, your Little Leaguer's physique.
We expected you to belt that ball right out of the park.

In the bleachers, we screamed your name till the other players'
families gave us the evil eye. It wasn't just a game to us.
We were the immigrant kids from that hijacking island.
We had something to prove.

You swung hard and fast, missing the ball altogether. A boy
on first, another on third. You could win this game, win it.
Your stance was good, bat high, but the ball flew right by you.

Easy out, easy out, the opposing team chanted. I joined in,
sotto voce. It was over, and everyone knew it. You lost,
and then you kept on losing.

QUEENS

We shamed you into leaving,

said you stank up the bathroom,
sprayed you with air freshener

until you choked.

You'd sneak off to E.J. Korvette's

to shit or wait till morning recess
at Catholic school where nobody

could blame just you.

Years later I learned this word
from a shrink: encopretic.

It means holding things in to bursting.
It means carrying the rage within.

DESEO #2

To unloose
>   the lost grace between us.

Bleach it milky white.

ADONIS

You returned from that summer in France so tanned and buff that the Brooklyn girls took notice. And it took a lot for the Brooklyn girls to take notice.

You were a god from spearfishing the Riviera: a sexy new language, microscopic red bathing trunks that no American boy would dare to wear.

The phone was ringing off the hook. As sister-of-Adonis, I was courted too. Gave the lovelorn advice on their chances with you. *Oui,* you were hot.

How we reveled in that brief August glory.

FIRST TIME

When the architect's son passed you that joint,
the coarse, hot smoke warmed your chest,
whispered: *Good boy, nice boy.* What you
desperately needed to hear.

It's unfashionable, probably irrational, to think
one joint undid you at twelve, led to homelessness
and crack. Isn't that something a Republican
would say?

PART II

1973–1994

DESEO #3

To turn back the clock,
        shield us from terror.

For this,
I would give my last song.

BROWNSTONE

Our last foot fight, thighs blazing,
Papi coming in to make us stop.

Soon after midnight the beatings began. I
heard your screams rise up from the basement
where fugitive
                slaves once hid. Mami

put him up to it,
put his macho on the line.

RESPUESTA

A word from you
      might've stopped it.

      You were good
with words.

KNIGHT

You were a merry young knight
in red tights and tunic,
you sang in the chorus and
danced a two-step with maidens.

In red tights and tunic
you cheered on your princess,
danced a two-step with maidens
with a modicum of polish.

You cheered on your princess
in my high school's spring play
with a modicum of polish,
barely clinging to dignity.

In my high school's spring play
you sang in the chorus and,
barely clinging to dignity,
you were a merry a young knight.

YOUR ROOM

Papi having another affair; Mami

lost in those damn love songs again (I'll hate
Julio Iglesias forever), disappeared

to South America for months only to
return and pretend she didn't remember

us. I never really believed her amnesia act
but she gave a performance worthy of a first-

rate Mexican *novela*. When I found her
in the closet covered with shoes, I promised

myself I would never let a man do
what he did to her. If this is love —

What I started out to say is
that we had two little dogs, affenpinschers that no

one looked after, or walked, only occasionally fed —
we were all in a terrible daze — and those dogs took

to shitting in your room,
where none of us ever went and

none of us bothered to clean, least of all you.
Chiquillos de mierda, Mami called us.

NEWSPAPERS

That rented room on State Street. Dirty
mattress on the floor. School uniform unused.
This was after you were kicked out of home.
I brought you leftover lasagna and two cans of soup.
I promised clean sheets, but never came back.

That winter I saw you bundling newspapers outside
the candy store. It was freezing and you had no gloves.
Your hands were pink hams. You waved, glad to see me,
and I waved back. I was on my way to school.

REPORT

Who: the girl next door

What: sex

When: her fourteenth summer

Where: her pink coverlet

Why: because you could

WHAT YOU DREAM

No one questions your judgment.
Someone else pays the bills.

You are pursued by mythic beasts
with mythic claws and mythic teeth.

They call you by your childhood
name. They know your secrets.

And threaten to tell them.

TRIP

A platoon of radiant aliens
      plays chutes and ladders on your thighs.
Watch them frolic!
Watch them slide!

Infrared warnings flash of contaminants
as you land hard.
      Time to refuel, earthling.

FLIGHT SCHOOL

You were too short for the Air Force by an inch (damn genes) so
you flew the private Cessnas. I imagine you soaring against the
clean northern skies, shredding clouds to oblivion.

Next thing I heard you were busted. Is it true what they said?
That you ran the biggest crack den in New England? Or were you
merely dealing coke to the rich Dartmouth boys?

Why am I telling this story, anyway?
Why don't you tell it instead?

BRAIN

Halved walnut halved
   again
        dusted with gunpowder.

Right lobe courts conceit, a flaunting evil.
   Its motto: *Nothing in nature says no.*

   The left lobe labors, motto-less, in the day-to-day hard light.
   Nothing rhythmical is permitted.

This contest was rigged from the beginning.

MUGGING

It was a cold night in New Hampshire and you
were looking for an easy mark.

An old woman, head to toe in black, a widow
maybe, hobbled down the street.

What did you imagine was in her huge, black
purse with the tarnished clasp?

A just-cashed Social Security check? Her month's
allotment of twenties?

You didn't expect her to put up a fight and when
she did, you dragged her ten feet.

By then passersby came to her rescue and some-
body called the police.

She didn't let go and neither did you.
Feisty broad pressed charges too.

You called our father from the county jail to bail
you out, but he didn't.

None of us did.

TWENTY-NINE PALMS

For years, I had an 8x10
Of you in your dress blues.

It was the third time
Since you were six

That you'd worn a uniform:
That time after Catholic school,

And then at the military academy
In Pennsylvania, where you learned

How to kill and hotwire cars
And endure discipline.

How did you take to the
Cold-turkey methods for

Daily everything? Did they
Make you feel at home?

You in the nowhere desert
Fixing weekend caravans

To get laid in L.A., racing
Sixteen tequila shots.

Coño, men with buzz cuts
Give me the creeps. Enough

With the *semper fi* postcards.
Get the hell out, already!

Eventually, you did, on a
Dishonorable discharge, another

Story I'm too weary to tell. And you,
With a lit match between your fingers.

A PASTORAL

Is no place for abstractions, like
feminism, which you have no use for.
Your natural habitat is idealism, '50s style,
an abstraction if there ever was one.

And you in the family restaurant
play-acting the maître d'. Twelve hours
a day on your feet then off to China-
town for the world's best noodles with
    garlic beef.
                Nothing abstract about that.

VIGILANTE

You drove a taxi strung out on crack,
made record time across Bed-Stuy.
Red lights only encouraged you.

The night shift was where you lived.
You knew every pickpocket's tricks, flashed on your
high beams, gave chase down alleyways

until you cornered the crooks.
No matter your terrified passengers.
You wanted to be one of the good guys.

Here's what you got instead: speeding tickets, insults,
more wounded pride, no tips.
Thank God you never bought a gun.

NAMESAKE

In other countries, Papi said,
children start working at five.

To work is to love.

In 1992, you opened a diner
in a piss-poor part of New Jersey.
You had big plans for your charbroiled burgers,
all the deep-fried flesh you loved.
You were open two months before you folded.

You're burning daylight.

Out of charity
or desperation,
you emptied the icebox
into the fryer,
all of it,
just for us.
Your sole employee
didn't know she'd
be jobless come morning.
I nibbled
the freezer-burned,
beer-battered shrimp,
hypnotized
by the giant neon sign
  blinking
your name,
    his name,
like a curse.

HIS BEST FRIEND

Your mother worked for my parents ordering
gift wrap and greeting cards. She went to Smith
and married your father, Amherst, Class of '59.
My father bought the bottom half of your mother's
brownstone, the one her father had given her.
It was difficult to feel superior but you tried.

Your family referred to my family as "tenants."
You didn't invite us to your Christmas sing-alongs.
Later, your father screwed his secretary and left
your mother in a scandalous scene the whole street saw.
Then your younger brother died of AIDS.
None of this was supposed to happen.

You'd look for my brother when you came home from
Amherst, Class of '82, and then again from Stanford Medical
School, where you trained as a pediatrician and met
your neurologist wife, a cold and beautiful landscape.

The last time you saw him, he asked you for money.
You gave him everything in your pockets: $186 plus change.
He said: Thanks, man. And: Take care of yourself.
You said: Same to you, man. Same to you.

GIRLFRIEND

You dated my brother for nearly two years.
He bought you a ring and said you'd be
married with kids before you turned thirty.

You met at an AA meeting. It was your
first time. Your drinking was off the charts —
everyone in your family's a drunk.

He passed you the sugar cookies and
said: I'm glad you're here. Then later:
I know I'm not supposed to ask you

your name but I want to take you to dinner.
How's that for a smooth opening? Cuban
boys are experts at smooth.

Soon you two were seeing each other. He
talked a good game and took care of you in that
way American men don't do anymore, plus

he was good in bed (you told me this), and you
thought: What more could I want? A lot
more, it turns out. He stole your credit

cards to buy you gifts and pay for your
trip to meet our family at Christmas.
When he begged for forgiveness, you took

him back but then he started using
again and there was no talking to him
when he was using so you said: *Adios, amigo.*

WHAT THEY FOUND

Barricaded in that rotting apartment
with the miniature dog I gave you —
you couldn't be reached by anybody.

There were sightings by other tenants,
mostly post-midnight, mostly alone.
Reports of Jimi Hendrix blasting
in the middle of the day.

In the men's department, nobody had seen
you either but the manager said you were
the best damn salesman they'd ever had.

When they finally broke down your door,
here's what they found: a hundred dress shirts
still in their plastic wrappers, a carton of Italian
silk ties, thousands of hours of pornography.

And the miniature dog I'd given you was living
on Cheetos and Dr. Pepper.

IN CUBAN

Nothing fit you the way it should: not brother,
not lover, not son. Certainly nothing in Cuban.

When you smoked, you forgot the toxic nostalgia
you had no use for, bogus histories in Cuban.

What you wanted were ties to the men who mattered
in Red Hook, not another whine-a-thon in Cuban.

You tried on variations of your name, anything
to distance yourself from your inheritance in Cuban.

But we come from a long line of skeptics and suicides,
borderline behaviors, all manifested in Cuban.

Who am I to guess at what you've suffered?
I am only your sister, Cristina, dreaming in Cuban.

SALVATION

The sickly smoke of church incense kindles deliverance
like a good crack pipe.

Immortality lasts forever. Transcendence switch hits.
But you knew that already.

Our sister tried to save you, tracked you down to crack
dens, bullied pushers.

When she finally gave up, it wasn't on you,
but on martyrdom.

PRINCETON

The invitation came from another university
to the north: a reading, a banquet in my honor.
Just the ticket for my postpartum blues.
I asked you to help me be a starlet for one night.
You agreed, for a fee: a hundred dollars cash plus
expenses. I didn't ask: What expenses?
Everything went wrong.
The car wouldn't start. I ran out of diapers.
Baby chose that moment to melt down.
I called and cancelled the whole shebang.
And you, you still took the cash.

DESEO #4

That you give up your religion,
the one thing that can still kick your ass.

That you grow quietly, devotedly happy.

RESPUESTA

It's too late for me and you.
Nothing's true except what the body
tells.
Enough with your lying geography.

SUNDAY

Winter is wretched here,
No amenities.
        The one bulb burnt out months ago.
Hands too stiff to ignite the pipe

Oh, to forgive what you once were before you became this.
Good ear listening to the forbidden.
        Fat woman howling in a red corset and heels.

Only this rock will bring redress,
        refinements.

        The harrowing light.

PART III

1995–2007

WINTER TAPESTRY

What's lived is gone, a blissful
hit. The last unraveled green.

I get your need now
for euphoria.
    Its half-breath from transcendence.

YOUR ADVICE

Lie,
  if you have to. (That's

  what I do.)

DISTASTE

Have you ever looked at his hands thick and calloused a worker's
hands how he eats with them makes me sick he's crude as a truck
driver honestly I don't know where he came from he doesn't feel
a part of me I don't believe for a minute that he's disabled bipolar
whatever he wants to call it you know what I think it's all an
excuse to avoid work I don't know where he came from he doesn't
feel a part of me I get so upset thinking about him it's bad for my
health he makes me overeat and fight with your father our biggest
fights are over him I don't know where he came from he doesn't
feel a part of me only a few of my closest friends know he exists
but they don't ask too many questions I get so angry when I think
about how he's wasted his life how he's ruined mine really I don't
know where he came from.

FRIED RICE

You tried to hack off your arm with a butcher's knife.
Your scar is frightening, your arm atrophied and dangling
a flap of skin. You click your dentures in and out,
can't remember much about it.

Long-ago memories are crystalline:
The spangly truck with Chinese food that came
around in summer. The tree house out back where you
waged wars with the court to the north.
The thirty-six times Mami hit you with a shoe.

Why can't I remember more
about you? The tens of thousands
of hours you've been my brother?

Your history is mine too.

TWELVE YEARS AGO

I was newly divorced and living in
a Spanish bungalow with a kitchen
I painted bright blue. Every room
was brilliant: salmon, lemon,
a deep abiding green. You came
for a long visit: stayed up nights
watching who-knows-what; hibernated
days away. Your niece refused to go near you.
Defecated on the kitchen floor. Wouldn't sleep alone.
Had nightmares when she did. I drove you to Santa Barbara
to break the news. I blamed the child psychologist,
her father-replacement theories.

Perhaps you never forgave me.
Perhaps you never should.

WEDDING

When our sister threw out the hairdresser who insisted that a '60s up-do
would make her a beautiful bride, where were you?

In the buzz of preparations at our parents' Brooklyn brownstone,
people asked: *Is he coming?*

On the streets during the day; at the men's shelter every night.
Weren't you afraid of people like you?

Our sister was heartbroken when you didn't show up. She craned her neck
around the guests. *Is he here yet?*

She believed in the magic of vows, as if making a promise were infectious,
like the mumps. Remember how we'd shared those?

LISTEN

What did he do to make you despise him? I don't mean later,
when he deserved it, but early on.

When he was barely a boy.

It's hard for him not to take it personally. He's your son. Born
after two welcomed girls.

Couldn't you have loved him a little?

I have a picture of you, fat and unlovely with—
excuse me—weird rhinestone glasses

at my second birthday party.

But there are no pictures of him as a baby.
Were they left behind in Cuba?

Do they exist at all?

By most accounts he was a quiet child, no bother to anyone. He's learned
a lot from his 942 therapy sessions.

Yes, each one has buried him

deeper in the hole you dug when he looked in your face and there was
no one looking back.

ODE

It sits there prettily, brownish rock
in my glass crack pipe. A hand-held torch
makes it snap and crackle into sweet
vapor I suck into my lungs,
into the hurt behind my eyes.

Sweet mother love shoots me skyward
burning high with the moon and Orion and all
the other heavenly dudes who orbit, orbit, orbit
Planet Earth. I am part of something big, man,
and I want to fuck the universe.

Yeah, my dick's a million light years long.
The hard-on would last forever, if only I had
the cash. But ten minutes of eternity is better
than any ordinary way to die.

POULTRY

It was your last hope: a chicken farm in the Florida
panhandle run by missionaries who bragged success
with men like you. Shoveling shit in the hot sun
would leave you too tired, they vowed, to want
to light up. You didn't understand "hardscrabble"
till then: the unyielding earth, the vicious pecking
order of the South. Plus the wet heat and bugs
nearly killed you.

    How long did you last? A week? Next I heard
you were doing time in a county jail for stealing
appliances. A hot plate is one thing but a refrigerator?
The missionaries, different ones, came around
for a year and a half, got you praising the Lord for
a while. Your last "Hallelujah!" expired your first
day out.

ANGELS

Evading the heavy-buttocked angels of temptation is a goddam full-time
job. No amount
      of befouling *mea culpas* or half-lit testimonials will purge them
      from your head.

They flit at you with crimped wings, promising conquest silver to make
it right this time.
      They know everything they need to strike the fever, get you
      naked and high.

Sweet sisters of ardor, make your wondrous case against oblivion. No
matter the
      omissions. I'm listening.

EL CLAVE

It is   easier
with you   from afar
hermano   mío.
Our sister   loses
sleep each   time she speaks
(one-two   cha-cha-chá)
with you   accuses:
blackmail!   aggression!
The thing   we fear most
is your   need because
there's no   end to it
and because   there's no
(turn-turn   step-step-step)
end to it   we fear
being   sucked in by
it and   (one-two-three)
absence   is a kind
of romance   when you
think about   it a
tremulous   calcu-
lation   for keeping
distances.   *Ay, sí.*

BIPOLAR

On the one hand, you
scheme and steal, feel
the energy of the stars
and nothing, nothing
can stop you from your
inner god. You are all
powerful, misunderstood,
and you will prove your
genius to everyone but
first you must sell the
most blood pressure
devices at the supermarket,
illustrate evil
with your poster boards
and charts, spend your
month's check on promotions
because no matter the
cost, you will succeed.

On the other hand, it's
hard to get out of bed
to face another muggy
a.m. with its handfuls of
medications and another
session with the shrink,
reliving your mother's
rejection. Yes, that's the
main issue here, reject-
ion and abandonment,
so why not surrender
to that fact and give
up on yourself entirely,
but you're too tired to
roll out of bed so you
dribble pee in a bottle
and think killing yourself
is too big an effort.

PRAYER

Lapsed Catholics can't go asking favors of demanding gods,
or the untidy forces of the universe.

But if anyone's out there, hear me out:

I have this brother, you see, who's tormented by simple things:
brushing his teeth, killing his Great Dane's fleas.

Is there anything you can do for him?

I'm willing to make the necessary sacrifices. Kill a black rooster.
Sprinkle its blood on sacred stones.

Would it take a pilgrimage? Just tell me where to go and what to
bring.
One more thing: Can I do this without talking to him?

DESEO #5

That you un-nail yourself
from your cross
                        draw up
        a manifesto for old age.

That after this cinematic life
                        you will
live simply again.
        .

RESPUESTA

Save your unburdenings, sister.
                    I've got enough problems
    as it is.

            Uneasy? Try tranquilizers.

REINCARNATED

I know what you're thinking.
That I'd probably choose some badass king of the jungle.
But you underestimate me.

I hate when you underestimate me.

As a matter of fact, I'd choose a nightingale.
I've never heard one sing but I know they keep
insomniacs company.

What do you know about me, anyway?

If I tell you I'd be a nightingale, believe it.
I happen to know that only unpaired males sing at night
and that they're iconic in Persian poetry.

You gonna steal that?

Don't pretend like suddenly you're this caring, concerned
person when all you're doing is using my shit.
Let me guess what you'd be, huh? A piranha?

ASCENSION

Here's my shortcut to heaven:

Loot your veins with high-grade junk (only the unholy best will
do).

Welcome the revelations.

                    Rise,
                         baby,
                              rise.

SHRINK

You say she's bipolar herself, knows about mood swings.
That once she spent $36,000 on designer shoes.

You notice the satin sheen on the high heels she's wearing.
You wonder if these are part of her cache.

She's devising new cocktails of drugs for you. She has religion
for fixing what's long been broken.

You get hard staring at her shiny new shoes.
It's been years since you touched anyone.

Do you have children? You stammer, dry-mouthed.

IN YOUR OTHER LIFE

You are in your prime. Teeth intact. A *pater-*
    familias. Two teenaged sons. They

respect you. I can't decide on your wife. She
    would probably be dark-eyed. Lebanese.

Like that dancer you loved as a boy. Curvy. Ample
    thighs. Years later, she visited my house.

What would you be doing? Something financial.
    High-risk arbitrage. A hedge fund.

Anything with tons of money. A sense of the edge.
    No art. Hardly a book. No music.

Maybe flying planes. Or jumping out of them.
    The better to appease your need for adventure.

I do not give you drugs. In your other life
    you did a little cocaine in the '80s without

crash-burning. Your relations with our parents
    are cordial. Formal. You show up to

holiday functions. Your polite family. Handsome.
    But the ghost of what's missing torments you.

A longing. For the other life you might've led.
    For the battered suitcase in flames.

FORGETTING

I'm not depressed like I hear you get,
wanting to blow your brains out, but a more-
of-the-same lifelessness that's getting me down.
Maybe I shouldn't be mucking through the past
like some sick archaeologist holding up
broken forks and making deductions. This
is our history we're talking about here, not
some ancient civilization we can opt out of.
Our parents are still alive and they're coming
to stay with me soon, and I want to be nice but
a part of me wants to read them these poems
and have them say, We were wrong, or
the thing they'll never say: We're sorry.
Well, *I'm* sorry, really sorry for hiding
out in these words instead of calling you and telling
you that I do remember and that it's much much
harder than forgetting.

SPELL

First, acknowledge your debt to those who came before you —
the uncle who hanged himself in Oriente,
our manic-depressive grandmother.
Florid, self-destructive relatives on both sides.

Next, admit that your unorthodox methods of survival
have failed. Then take a ball of red yarn
dipped in kerosene and wrap it slowly
around your naked body, feet first, moving upward.

Fall to your knees. Light the yarn, then tilt
your head back till you face the sky and beg
for redemption. Receive the loaves of bread
floating down like answered prayers to feed you.

Partake of the bread. When you have eaten
your fill, run a cool bath. Regret freely.

BULK

Some days you can't reach down to scratch your balls.
They hardly get blue anymore with all those medications
    you're taking.
(Your bones are nowhere in evidence, only the hideous peek-a-boo
feet, calcifying; damn lapsing decorum of flesh.)

Curse the old rank hungers, insistent as trolls.
The air around you is spent,
                    recycling ripened lungs.
What you need now is to pure your want down
                                  to zero.

APOLOGIA

You weren't invited to their anniversary party
at the seaside resort with the cameraman
and the two-piece band. Septuagenarians—nips,
tucks, and new hips—dance the mambo and cha-cha.

A generous buffet of fatty meats and fettuccine
Alfredo, a sundae bar with chocolate syrup
spigots.

How do they get to fifty eating like this?

You weren't invited because you:

a) *couldn't handle it*
b) would be overwhelmed by the opulence
lacking in your no-frills existence and (possibly
dangerously) incited to spite
c) would make their friends feel uncomfortable:
your 1. size, 2. dentures, 3. family resemblance. Plus
a lot of them don't know you exist.
What son?
d) cause shame

You weren't invited to their anniversary party.

So we, your sisters, ate the fatty meats and drank
champagne and made excuses for you. We raised
our glasses and wished them
                another fifty years.

You weren't invited, *hermano*, but you
got this poem instead.

WHEN YOU DIE

When you die, we will scrape our knees
on the Stations of the Cross, shave our heads,
lament: *¡Ay, que pena!*

He was a talented boy, street-smart, a go-getter.
He could charm a herd of buffalo
to stampede his way.

But you're alive, sick and unacknowledged,
suicidal, unmourned. You would talk to us twelve
hours a day if you could.

So what are we waiting for, *hermano*?
The lesser tragedy of death?

Coda

LAST DREAM

You are transparent, a crisp plastic model of man,
        and you carry a trumpet.

The conical heart is placed obliquely in the chest,
        five inches long, eons old.

You turn. A sudden refraction
        of light reveals the muscles of the soft
        palate,
            the pharynx laid open from behind.

Soft lobes are everywhere: in your brain, in
        your liver, in your honeycombed
        lungs.

You are impressed by the articulative possibilities
        of the wrist, the grave interlock
            of pelvis with hip
        (the future of humanity depends upon this).

You find the texture of your fat oddly compelling.

Of special note: the whispering cavity of the tympanum,
        the colon,
            ascending and descending.

You crave the sticky pulsing of the carotid.
            You bring the trumpet to your lips.